ISBN 0 9517930 0 4

**Acknowledgements:** *I would like to thank the students of memory whose research has helped to stimulate some of the ideas in this booklet, and the neurological patients whose memory disorders have provided such insights into memory functioning.*

# What is Memory?

## Different Types of Memory

There are different types of memory skills rather than a single memory ability. For example, remembering what someone has said involves a different type of memory than trying to remember someone's face. Also, remembering something that happened a short time ago is different from the memory that is involved in recalling how to drive a car.

 Memory for skills such as driving a car may often be unaffected in people with everyday memory difficulties.

Remembering things that happened many years ago is usually easier than remembering something that happened yesterday, partly because older memories tend to be rehearsed over and over again and may be specially important for someone.

# Different Stages of Remembering

LEARNING
STORAGE
RECALL

When we remember something for the first time, there are usually three stages involved — the *learning* stage, which deals with what happens when we first concentrate on something for the first time — the *storage* stage, where things we've tried to learn are somehow stored in the brain — and the *recall* stage, when we try to bring to mind what we've learned. If any of these stages is affected, then a memory lapse may occur. While there is often little we can do to improve the *storage* stage of memory, we can sometimes do something about the *learning* and *recall* stages.

Much of this manual is about offering advice and suggestions as to how you may try to improve your learning and recall skills.

# Things to Bear in Mind

*Firstly*, no one's memory is perfect! We all tend to forget things from time to time, and what we keep in memory will often depend on how keen we are on remembering the thing in question, how interesting we think it is, etc. You may well find you are now more aware of memory lapses, but it is important to realise that your memory was never perfect. You shouldn't say things to yourself such as *"I can't remember anything"* or *"I'm stupid, I'm always forgetting things"* because this may make you feel that your memory is worse than it actually is. If you really *are* forgetful lots of times, try to keep a sense of humour about it.

*Secondly*, if you are under stress or anxiety then this is likely to have a bad effect on your memory.

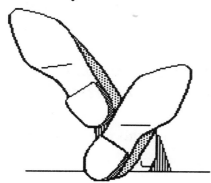

You may find that if you are more relaxed about things and make your life-style more easy-going, this itself may help to improve your memory.

*Thirdly*, a poor memory is sometimes the result of poor concentration or trying to do too many things at once. When you are doing one thing, try to concentrate on it and not let your mind wander on to other things. You will learn best in a place that is relatively free of distractions. If you are interrupted while doing something, try to go back to it as soon as possible afterwards.

*Fourthly*, try to be well organized in your everyday routine. This may mean only doing certain things at certain times of the day or on certain days of the week, putting things away/ filing things carefully in their own place, not allowing the place where you work or live to get cluttered, etc.

This booklet is intended to be a general guide to ways of improving memory, and not a "cure" for memory problems. At the moment, no one knows for sure of any treatment which will result in a huge change in someone's memory.

Do not worry if you find some of the ideas described in the booklet more attractive than others - memory strategies and memory aids that suit one person may not necessarily suit someone else.

In this manual, we'll be talking about four

main ways in which you can help to improve your memory —

- **Using Simple Aids**
- **Learning in Better Ways**
- **Recalling in Better Ways**
- **Practising Some Memory Activities**

Try to get into the habit of using more than one of these ways at any particular time. If you do some of the practice games, try to make them as similar as possible to everyday memory situations. And remember, practising for one type of memory skill may not necessarily result in an improvement for other types of memory skill. *The important thing about the practice games is to use them as a chance to try out the various ideas for improving memory which have been described elsewhere in the manual.*
We won't be covering all possible memory problems — there just wouldn't be room — but some of the ideas can be tried in other types of memory situations.

# Remembering People's Names

## Learning in Better Ways

When you meet someone for the first time, listen carefully to their name. If it's an unusual name ask them to spell it for you. Think for a moment whether or not you like that particular name. If you are introduced to several people, try to make an excuse to repeat their names back to them (e.g. *"Let me be sure I've got your names right"*). Try to use the name as often as possible in your initial conversation (e.g. *"I'm glad to meet you, John"*). It will probably help if you repeat the name again after

a short interval, say after a few minutes, rather than immediately, as this will also help to make it stick better in your mind. You may feel strange saying the person's name again and again in a conversation, but most people enjoy hearing their name being spoken!

If you can get some sort of meaning from the person's name, this will help you to remember it better. In the case of a foreign name, you may have to alter the way it sounds to make it more meaningful (e.g. *Mustafa* can become *Must Have A*), and a long name is best split up into shorter words. In some cases, the name may be easy to picture in your mind as something else (e.g. Mr. Butcher), but in other cases you may have to twist the name slightly to make it sound more meaningful, e.g. *jam* for 'James' and *cone* for 'Cohen'.

If you are trying to remember both the first and second names, or the names of a couple of people, you may find it useful to form a word (one that you can easily picture) from the initial letters of the two names — e.g. for *James Cohen*, you could form the word *JuiCe*, and imagine the person drinking lots of juice, or for *Mary* and *Peter*, you could make up the word *MoP*, and imagine them both mopping the floor together.

One technique which people sometimes use to help associate a name with a face is to make an unusual link between a mental image and the person's name - e.g. if the person's name was James Cohen, you could imagine him eating from an ice-cream cone with jam on the top, and so when you meet the person next you would think of jam on an ice-cream cone and then think of the name James ('jam') Cohen ('cone')!

Don't worry about making up an unusual picture — the more unusual it is, the better the name will stick in your memory.

If the person has something unusual about his appearance you could associate this with his name — e.g. in the case of a Mr. Cohen if he has a beard you could imagine the beard being in the shape of a cone. In general, concentrating on anything unusual about the person's face, or thinking how attractive the face is to you, should help to make it stick better in your memory, whether you want to remember their name or just that you've seen them before. Remember to concentrate on their face or physical appearance, rather than on things such as their dress/hair-style, as these can change over time!

It may also be helpful to link the person with someone who has the same name and whom you know well — this could be one of your friends or a famous personality. If you already know someone of the same name, try to think of some similarities — e.g. in appearance or occupation — between the person you are meeting for the first time and the other one you already know well.

When you say good-bye to someone, try to make it a habit of saying their name again (e.g. *"It was nice meeting you, John"*). Try to recall their face and name a short time later, and try to do this if possible every few hours and over the next few days.

If you used any technique for learning to associate the face with the name, try to think of the same one when you are rehearsing it in your mind.

## Recalling in Better Ways

When you are in a situation where you cannot remember a person's name, try not to panic! Try going through possible names beginning with each letter of the alphabet. Think of the situation where you first learned the name and anything about the situation which you may have linked with the name. Don't give up immediately after trying to remember the name — if you try again later, it may come back to you.

If after trying a number of times you still can't recall the name, don't be afraid to ask the person his/her name — you could say something like *"I remember you very well, but your name has slipped my mind for the moment!"*. Or, you

could say your own name as you shake hands with the person.

He or she may instinctively do the same when they shake hands with you.

Finally, don't forget that you can often have a friendly chat with someone without actually saying their name!

## Memory Practice

You can always practise how well you remember people's names by cutting out photographs from magazines or newspapers, giving the person any name you like and trying to remember the names a number of times. You could do this in the form of a game of 'matching pairs' — paste a set of photos of faces on to cards, with the names on the back of the cards. Make up two sets. Put one set on the table with the faces looking up, and the other set with the names looking up. Pick a face card, and then try to find the name card which has the same face on the other side. You could play this game with some friends or even with children. It would probably be useful to start off with three faces and then gradually work up to five or six faces. When you are doing any sort of practice, it is also useful to retest your memory for the names by coming back to the photographs after half an 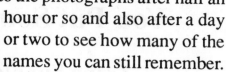 hour or so and also after a day or two to see how many of the names you can still remember.

*Remember to try out some of the memory aids and hints that were described earlier.*

# Remembering Where You Put Something

## Using Simple Aids

Try to be well organized about where you put things. Spend some time (e.g. half an hour each Monday morning) making things a little more organized and putting back things which may have got out of place. Have set places in your home/office for specific things you use — e.g. everyday things (keys, purse, glasses, etc.), mail, money items. Try to get into the habit of putting things away carefully and returning them to their proper place after use. Keep a separate place for things you need to remember to do or take with you every day, and make sure this place stands out in your line of view.

Make a list of those things which you tend to lose quite often, and make it a special habit to put them away carefully, label them if necessary, etc. It may also help to write down a list of the places where you tend to keep different things, to have this list readily at hand and to use it each time you put something away. It can be helpful to put labels onto cupboards or jars where you tend to keep particular things. For keeping small things, you might find it handy to have a plastic, transparent storage unit with its own little drawers — such as you find in hardware or DIY stores.

You might also think of putting self-adhesive labels (with your name, address and telephone number) on certain things, such as umbrellas or books, that you tend to leave lying around.

If you are going outside, try to carry things all together in a bag or brief-case, or attach them to part of your clothing — this way, you will be less likely to lose something by leaving it some-where and forgetting where you have put it. Also, if you sit down and put something like an umbrella or a bag near you, put it in front of you so that you can easily see it — you are then less likely to leave it behind. If you are carrying several things around with you, keep in your mind the number of things you have, and then check from time to time that you still have that number.

## Learning in Better Ways

Stop and think each time you put something away. Concentrate for a few seconds and look at the particular place where you put the thing. Also, try to give yourself a reason why you are putting the thing in a particular place. Better still, try to form a connection between the thing in question and the place where you are putting it. For example, if you put a key in a cup try to imagine yourself drinking with a large key in your hand rather than a cup! When the time

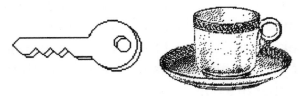

comes for you to try to remember where you put the key, then you should at the same time think of the cup and this will help you remember where you put the key.

If you are parking your car in a large car park, try to remember the position of the car compared to something such as the exit or a ticket machine — and the number of the floor if you are on a multi-storey car park. When you are walking away from you car, glance back at it a few times and concentrate on where you left it.

Once you've put something away, try to think of it, and where you put it, at intervals afterwards. Try to make these intervals a little longer each time.

# Recalling in Better Ways

If you have difficulty in finding something which you have put away some time earlier, try to go back in your own mind to when you last remember having the thing. Then, go through step by step what you did and where you were after that.

You can also pretend that you are putting the thing away again for the first time, and think of the likely places you would put it.

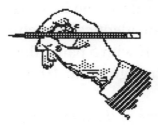 Writing down all the likely places on a piece of paper may also help.

It is often helpful to first of all look very carefully in the most likely places, and later on look in the less likely places.

It can sometimes be very frustrating if you cannot find something that you put away. If you still cannot find it after searching, try to pause and relax for a few minutes. Ask yourself how important the thing really is — can you buy or make do with something else for the time being, or is there someone who can lend you one?

# Memory Practice

You could put half a dozen objects in different places last thing before you go to bed, write down on a piece of paper where you put them, and the next morning try to discover where they all are without looking at the paper. See how many you can get right.

A children's game which people often find both enjoyable and stimulating (one you can find in most toy shops) is 'matching pairs' — lots of pictures are laid face down, and you have to try to pick up a pair of identical matching pictures. You could start off with 5 pairs (that is 10 pictures in all), and then go on to 10 pairs, then 15 pairs, etc.

*Remember to try out some of the memory aids and hints that were described earlier.*

# Remembering To Do Something

## Using Simple Aids

It is usually helpful to have little 'prompts' which will help to remind you of things you have to do. For example, if you have to take something from home to get repaired, leave it in the front hall so that you can't help but see it when you leave the house. Some people find that they may remember to do something during the day if they have an unusual reminder in their view most of the time, such as a watch on the wrong wrist or a rubber band round a finger.

 If you are in your office, and need to remember to do something when you get home, curl part of your tie or other bit of clothing so that it sticks when you try to take it off after you reach home.

It is possible to buy watches, 'organizers', or portable-computers which can give an alarm at set times, and these can help you remember to do things like take tablets regularly. It helps if you can try to associate the thing in question with the actual sound of the alarm, for you may find when the alarm goes off you have forgotten what the reminder was for! For example, if you want to remember to post a letter, picture your alarm in the shape of a postage stamp — when  the alarm goes off, you will then be likely to think of the stamp, and that will remind you to post the letter. It is also now possible to buy 'electronic organizers' in which you can write down things you have to do — when the alarm goes off, they will show the message you wrote down. You can also buy pill-boxes, with the days of the week written on them, to help you remember to take tablets regularly.

Try to get into the habit of doing things *immediately* rather than after a while — if you leave things till later, you are more likely to forget to do them. If you have to do several things at around the same time, count them up and remember the number — if you count them off as you do them, you are less likely to leave one undone. Keep a pencil and paper handy at your bedside in case you suddenly think of something important you have to do during the night. If you don't have these at hand, put something such as a watch or pillow in an unusual position near your bed or pull out a bedside drawer, so that when you wake up you will realise that there is something you have to remember to do. In the morning, attend to this thing immediately you get up, otherwise you are likely to forget about it in the morning rush.

Keeping a diary, a wall-chart or wall-calendar is an obvious help in remembering to do something. If you keep a wall-calendar, hang it somewhere you look at most times of the day. If there's something you need to do everyday, such as take a medicine, you could write *M* on each day immediately after you take it. If there is a list of birthdays/anniversaries you need to remember, stick it next to the calendar.

Writing things down on a piece of paper or a little notebook which you have in front of you, or which you carry around, is also something which most people find useful. For some things, you could use the back of your cheque book to write on. It is important, when you think of something you have to do later on, that you write that thing down immediately in your diary or notebook rather than leaving it to another time. When you write down several things that you have to do, try to arrange them into meaningful groups, or try and find some sort of association between them.

If you have a list of things which you have to do, make sure the list is put in a place where you can easily see it — for example in the kitchen, if you are at home — or on your office desk, if you are at work. In general, it is useful to link the thing you have to do with something you already do by habit. For example, if you want to remember to take a letter with you to work, put it on the front door-handle or somewhere similar where it will easily stand out or next to something which you will be bound to take with you, such as your coat, brief-case, handbag, etc. Or, if you always look in the hall mirror before you go out, stick a note on the mirror or write a message on the mirror with lipstick to remind you to take the thing with you. If you are going on holiday somewhere, write down a list of things you have to take. Tick off the things as you pack them, and take a final look at the list when you are about to leave home. If you are often leaving things behind at home, put a note permanently on the mirror or the front door to remind you to take everything with you. If you need to remember to take some tablets, do it after something you regularly do — brushing your teeth in the morning, watching a TV program in the evening, etc. or keep the tablets near your toothbrush/ television to jog your memory. In general, try to get into a routine to do things at set times in the day — perhaps with one thing always following on from another — and on set days of the week.

# Learning in Better Ways

When you are thinking about something you have to do, try to get into the habit of saying it over to yourself several times. It may also be useful to picture in your mind the situation where you have to do the particular thing in question and to associate this with another thing which you are going to do.

For example, if you have to remember to go to the bakery after you go to the bank, make up a picture in your mind of the bank clerk giving you a cake instead of money! If you have to go to quite a few places, try first to combine them

into sets of two or three places, and then think up some links that connect the places in each set.

You could also associate something you must remember to do with something that happens regularly around the same time — like the arrival of the post/mail. You could make some connection between letters/parcels and the thing you have to do, so that one event will trigger your memory for the other. Similarly, if you have a number of things you have to say — as in a short speech you have to make — try to make some link between them.

If you have a long list of things to get, for example food to buy in a supermarket, and you don't have time to write things down on a piece of paper, try to group them together in some meaningful way — e.g. cheese, milk and butter could go together, vegetables and fruit together, etc. You could group items according to their size or their colour. Or you could think of the places in the supermarket where they are kept and try to link together those that are kept in the same area.

If you have to remember to do something in a particular place, picture the place in your mind and imagine doing the thing in question — e.g. if you have to remember to post a letter when you are near a shop, imagine the shop and picture yourself posting the letter when you are walking outside the shop.

Sometimes it's easy to forget something after even a few seconds — e.g. a toast you put back in the toaster. Try counting to five or ten slowly. By the time you have reached the number, it should be time to check the toaster again.

Try to get into the habit of regularly thinking about things you have to do. This way, you are more likely to keep them in your mind. If you go over such things at set times, for example when you start work in the morning, after lunch, etc. this will help you to keep them in your mind so that they are less likely to be forgotten.

# Recalling in Better Ways

Usually you will be unaware at the particular time that you have forgotten to do something — however, you may find that you realise that there was something you have to do but have forgotten what exactly it was. If you find yourself in this type of situation, stop and think for a moment about similar things you have to do — e.g. if you are out shopping, think of other bits of shopping you were supposed to get. Try also to think back to the situation where you first thought about doing the thing in question, or — if it is possible — go back to the place where you first decided to do the particular thing.

People often forget whether or not they have done a particular thing (e.g. shut a window, turned off an oven). One way to help this type of memory is to say aloud what you are doing at the time you are doing it — so when you are shutting the window, say *"That's the window shut"*.

# Memory Practice

Give yourself a list of three things to do, write them down somewhere, set an alarm for one hour later, and when the alarm goes off try to remember what they were. You can make this sort of exercise more difficult by increasing the number of things you have to do, increasing the length of time before you have to do something, and leaving out the alarm (though you need to have someone else to remind you just in case you forget!).

*Remember to try out some of the memory aids and hints that were described earlier.*

# Remembering What People Tell You

## Using Simple Aids

Writing down a message is an obvious aid. You may even find a pocket cassette recorder or electronic organizer handy for keeping a record of any messages. When you write things down, try to do this in an organized, meaningful way. Thus, you could split a long message under several main headings, you could number these and perhaps put sub-headings within each main heading. You could also make parts of the message stand out by simple techniques such as underlining, using capital letters or different coloured ink for important parts.

## Learning in Better Ways

 Try to think about what you hear — ask yourself questions such as whether you agree/disagree with it. When you remember numbers, try to join them into a group (e.g. remember 3-7-4 not as 'three-seven-four'

but as 'three hundred and seventy four'). In the case of a long telephone number you may find it useful to split the number into two parts — e.g. you could try to remember a number such as 193852 as "one hundred and ninety three" and "eight hundred and fifty two", or you could think of it as the year before the beginning of World War II (1938) together with the number of weeks in the year (52). Similarly, 430 could be remembered as tea-time (4.30 pm). Grouping numbers together like this or finding meaning in them makes them more likely to stick in your mind.

In the case of a list of things, a useful technique is to form a word from the first letters of the items. For example, if you had to remember to buy *B*read, *E*ggs, *D*ates and *S*oap you could form a word out of the first letters of the items. Such a 'key word' could be "BEDS". Then, by simply going through the first letters of the 'key word', you could recall each of the things. It might also be useful to actually associate the 'key word' with the place you are going to, so that you don't forget what you learned the 'key word' for. In this example, you could make a picture in your mind of some beds in front of the entrance to the supermarket you were going to.

Another similar idea is to form links between the words in a list. So if you had to remember to buy *bread, eggs, dates* and *soap*, you could imagine yourself making an *egg sandwich*, cracking open an *egg* only to find *dates* inside, and washing your face with *dates*! So, when you think of one thing you will immediately tend to think of the other. As we mentioned earlier, don't worry if the associations seem rather unusual - in general, the more unusual the association the more likely that it will stick in your memory.

An idea which you may find useful is to repeat the message several times, and, if possible, at intervals after you have initially heard it.

 Repeating it immediately afterwards will be useful, especially to make sure you were listening carefully and you heard it properly, but it is usually better if you repeat the message after an interval during which you have been doing something else. Of course, you may well find that if you try to repeat it after too long a time you will actually have forgotten part of it, so it may be useful to have it written down just in case, and to arrange the intervals so that they only gradually increase in length.

# Recalling in Better Ways

If you find that you have forgotten a particular message which has been given to you, try and think about other things about the message — who gave it, where it was given, what you were doing at the time, etc. You may find that this helps to bring back the thing to your mind.

# Memory Practice

Try to get someone to give you a list of things, for example a shopping list, and then to ask you half an hour later what was on the list. You could try similar exercises using telephone numbers, where your memory is tested over a short interval, so for example someone could give you a number to remember, then occupy your attention for about half a minute or so, and then ask you what the number was.

*Remember to try out some of the memory aids and hints that were described earlier.*

# Remembering What You Are Reading

## Using Simple Aids

If you are reading as part of a course of studies, you need to organize and space your study time sensibly. Some general hints include reading difficult material when you are fairly fresh and in your best state of mind, reading the same material but from different books, etc.

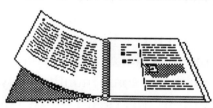

In general, it is useful to organize reading material into headings and to arrange the headings into meaningful groups so that some headings are related to each other. You may also find that you can make sub-headings and arrange these together in a similar way. Try to go over this group of headings each time you read the material.

## Learning in Better Ways

Before you read the material in depth try to glance through it first or if possible read a short summary of the information. Read the material again, keeping in mind the headings you have made. Try to relate different parts of the reading material to each other, and also to other, similar material which you already know well. Try to put the material into your own words as much as possible, and if you can also draw diagrams/ pictures to help you understand the material, so much the better. Colouring over key sentences with a 'highlighter' pen may also be helpful.

Test your recall of the information which you have just read, and try to repeat this after certain intervals which gradually increase in length. Read through it again, see what you have left out, and concentrate on this a little more when you go back over the material again. If you are studying for an exam that is some months away, it is sometimes useful to 'overlearn' what you are reading - this way, it is more likely to stick in your mind, even if you don't get a chance to look at it again in the meantime.

## Recalling in Better Ways

If you try to remember the information using the same technique you used when you learned it — that is with several headings which are related to each other — then you may find that everything fits into place a lot easier. Some people find it useful to think of the book-pages/ notes which they actually looked at, or the room in which they studied, if they are trying to recall something they read some time ago.

# Memory Practice

An exercise which you may find useful is to take a short story from a newspaper, read it several times, and test your memory for it.

 Do this with the same story until you are able to remember most of it. It is also important in the case of such an exercise to test your long-term memory for the information, that is, come back a day or so later and see how much of the particular story you can remember.

*Remember to try some of the memory aids and hints that were described earlier.*

# Remembering How To Get Somewhere

## Using Simple Aids

Having the directions on a clear map is obviously important. Make sure you go over this *before* you set out, and plan any long journey in stages. Landmarks such as hospitals are usually indicated on road maps, and you may find it useful to make a note of these. Some people prefer an actual map of the directions, others prefer the directions written on a piece of paper — choose the one you are happiest with and keep to it.

Find out if there is a road sign pointing to a particular place which you can follow — it is usually easier to do this than following directions to turn right and left several times. Before you set out, it is also wise to take along with you the telephone number of the destination to which you are heading, in case you have to ring them for further directions.

If you have difficulty in finding your way around a large house, try putting some sticky paper (e.g. coloured shapes) on the floor or arrows on the wall, with the names of the important places written on the markers. You may also wish to put labels on the doors of some of the rooms.

# Learning in Better Ways

If the directions you have to follow are quite long, try to split them up into shorter directions and concentrate on one direction at a time. If someone has told you the directions, repeat back what the person has said to make sure you got it right, and also if possible at intervals after that. Picture in your mind going in the particular direction you were given. Ask the person if there is a sign to a particular town which is in the same direction as your destination, as this will be easier to follow than a set of turnings. If you are going somewhere on foot, look back a few times at various landmarks so that when you are returning you will be able to recognize places more easily on your return journey. If you are going by car, you could do the same by looking in your mirror a few times.

If you are trying to learn your way around a new town, try to compare the lay out of the streets with somewhere you are familiar with, e.g. a place you previously lived in.

# Recalling in Better Ways

If you get lost or have difficulty in following some directions, stay calm and don't panic — just try to work through the directions you have already followed and try to think what are the other ways you could go. If you have been to your destination before, spend a few minutes thinking back to the directions you followed then.

Finally, don't be afraid to ask someone — e.g. at a petrol station — for the directions or to ring up the place you are heading for.

# Memory Practice

If you regularly go on a certain journey, e.g. when shopping, try going by an unfamiliar route on one occasion. Giving yourself practice in this way should help to improve your ability to find your way about and also make you more confident when you suddenly find yourself in a new situation.

*Remember to try out some of the memory aids and hints that were described earlier.*

# Memory Aids

*Here are a list of 25 everyday memory aids, some of which you may find helpful in your particular daily routine*

1. Make written checklists on memo self-stick notepads

2. Write things down in a pocket note-book

3. Write things down in a diary/filofax

4. Write messages down on the back of a cheque book

5. Write things down on a memo pad hanging on a cupboard/door

6. Write things down on a wall-chart or calendar

7. Use a diary-desk pad on your office desk

8. Leave something in a prominent place so that it acts as a prompt

9. Change part of your personal make-up, e.g. put a ring/watch/wallet in a different position than usual so that it acts as a prompt

10. Use a data watch alarm

11. Use an alarm clock/radio-alarm clock

12. Use a count-down timer

13. Use an electronic organizer

14. Use 'alarm' or 'diary' software on a portable or desk-top computer

15. Have inbuilt electronic memory aids in your car which give visual or auditory alarm signals

16. Use an electronic pill reminder or pill boxes/ containers to help you remember to take your medicine

17. Do something before/after some regular event during the day, e.g. after a TV programme, after a meal

18. Use a tape recorder/dictaphone as a memory aid

19. Use a memory phone to help your dial frequently used numbers. Using a phone with a digital display also means that you can see the numbers you are entering, making it less likely that you will make a mistake

20.    Use a portable telephone dialer to help you dial numbers

21.    Stick name labels on your possessions to help others return them if they get lost

22.    Use a remote control sonic/infra red detection device to help locate things - those for cars are fairly reliable, though most of the ones which can be used around the home are rather temperamental

23.    Put yellow velcro pads on the back of something to attach it to set places where you have stuck a white velcro cushion - this will encourage you to put things away in their proper place

24.    Stick yellow velcro pads or something with a rough edge onto objects or places so that you can find them by touch in the dark or while you are driving

25.    Ask a relative or friend to remind you about things

---

A Memory Aids Catalogue is available from — *Memory Aids Unit, Wessex Neurological Centre, Southampton General Hospital, Southampton SO9 4XY, England.*
Please enclose a cheque for £1.00 payable to *Wessex Neurological Centre* (or two US dollar bills if the request is from overseas).

# Notes